"Y"

A PLAY BY

PAULIE THE BALLIE

Copyright © 2020 by Paulie The Ballie.

ISBN   Softcover   978-1-951469-59-7

All rights reserved. No part of this book may be reproduced or transmitted in any form or by any means, electronic or mechanical, including photocopying, recording, or by any information storage and retrieval system without express written permission from the author, except in the case of brief quotations embodied in critical reviews and certain other non-commercial uses permitted by copyright law.

Printed in the United States of America.

To order additional copies of this book, contact:
Bookwhip
1-855-339-3589
https://www.bookwhip.com

The "Y" is dedicated to all shooting victims who have been taken from us. Some who have just started their journey. Their blood is still on our hands and we need to honor that loss with a renaissance in the way we look upon gun control, permitting weapons of war to be readily accessible. Taking assault weapons off our streets must be done without delay. 2. Everyone who purchases a gun must be checked out with a universal background check no exceptions. We need to support group's like Ban Assault weapons, Now.com So I am offering a free copy of play "Y" to anyone who contributes to Ban.

This writer had a vision back on 2/21/18 when two young Lass's came in to view directly before me after just awakening from a nap. They were looking directly at me with interest and I sensed they were there to encourage my humble efforts to write about those shooting tragedy's.

CONTENTS

Foreword vii
Introduction to "Y" xi

Scene 1:   The Debate 1
Scene 2:   Great Grand Pappy's Service during Civil War 5
Scene 3:   Battle of Little Big Horn Crow, Mt. 9
Scene 4:   Wild Bill Show out West 12
Scene 5:   Mandalay Hotel Room facing out to front of hotel 14
Scene 6:   Compartment on train leaving from Essex, England ... 16
Scene 7:   Bubba and Arthur Miller on stage for a talk 19
Scene 8:   Bubba shares some thoughts 25
Scene 9:   Bubba's reads his letter for his Young Readers 28
Scene 10: Bubba Shares his Pain 30
Scene 11: Bubba's conclusion and says So Long for now 33
Scene 12: After Thought: Bubba talks with Harriet
           Tubman center stage 35
Scene 13: Pops and Bubba have a serious talk 38
Scene 14: O Peace recited by Bubba who dedicates it to
           Benjamin Ferencz 41
Scene 15: Crossroads read by Bubba 44

Author's Bio 49

FOREWORD

This play is a three-fold effort: 1. A case for reparations for 90 years of slavery for 4,000,000. 2. The need to ban assault weapons 3. A possible answer to why humanity exists and what our destiny may be. + A letter for my young readers.

In Loving Memory of: John J. O'Mara An Irish Blessing: May the road rise to meet you. May the wind be always at your back. May the sunshine warm Your face, the rain falls soft upon your fields. And until we meet again may God hold you in the palm of His Hand. Amen

INTRODUCTION TO "Y"

Okay let's tell the folks about our Play. First let's start with a general approach to the theme of this play. Just a surmise about why we are here and what may be our destiny. Plus, the need to ban assault weapons.

I have found some interesting signs to reinforce the notion of a Determiner of Our Destiny. From all indications several scientific (In 1997 scientists created matter from light at the Stanford Linear Accelerator Center) recent experiments have shown that matter can be indeed created with certain elements and that this could explain how the universe came to be. Let's assume that space has always been here. No start, no end. It stretches forever with countless universes inter-connected and subject to the same law of physics. The very force of creation becomes mostly due to exploding stars and the debris that emanates from that form's gases that come together in space to create planets and their satellites. This creation is endless and goes on and on for infinity. The definite laws to govern this process is crying out for a divine overlord. Humanity has grasped this concept with open arms. Several religions clamor for the truth and yes, they all have the feeling of grace which has become a force that is unwavering and has survived for hundreds of years. So maybe it is our mission to explore and travel to far distant planets for colonization. That could be why we are here. Could it be our mission to transfer our DNA to the rest of the Universe? Hang on to your seats Folks as it is going to be one heck of a ride. Now back to Bubba and Pops.

SCENE 1

THE DEBATE

The need to start talking and come together is so needed today. Bubba has suggested let's get the two opposing views together for a Debate; So here it is: This is a 21st Century story about two different political philosophies. Far right hard line positions with the following mandate of as little government as possible. On the other end an ultra-liberal position that leaving the welfare all people to the private sector is dangerous with serious consequences with the economy. Which of these is for real and why so many peoples have both philosophies are the subject to this debate? One can only submit that the gridlock with Congress needs to move away from those two extremes and start to move towards the middle with a more pragmatic approach to finally get something done to move the Nation forward. We cannot continue with this gridlock. Too many things need tending to Infrastructure repair and passing a suitable single payer Health Insurance Program and raising the minimum wage to a more suitable figure of $15 per hour is our most demanding problems that need immediate attention.

Chapter – the Confrontation: It was the first of 4 debates concerning what policies are needed to meet the challenges of the 21st Century.

It will be shown by the three Networks. Representing the Far-Right Position was a young Tea Party Rep who recently lost his congressional Seat in the House. His name is Victor. Victor was raised in Lawrence, Kansas. He attended the University of Tulsa and is a devout Southern Baptist. He is 22 years of age. Representing the Ultra Liberals is Murray also 22 years of age. He attended Colombia Law and was just admitted to the New York Bar Association as one of the youngest to do so.

So, lets tune in to the Monitor who is about to start the debate. He says, "Okay, gentlemen each will make an opening statement with a tie limit of 5 minutes, and then several questions from myself and the audience will follow each answer will not exceed 3 minutes. Aside no clapping will be permitted. Let's keep it civil, Gentlemen as this will be during prime time on all three networks. Good Luck and we will start with Victor.

Howdy Folks, I am really honored to be here and want to thank the World Media Association for this invitation. First, this great nation was built on individual efforts and had to be done from the ground up. The development of our resources came about with good old fashion pure sweat and a dedication to create something that moves our Country forward. These accomplishments are part of our History and we showed to the World in the 20th Century how to foster a prosperous and rewarding economy with hard work by individuals. I will attempt to show that this initiative must be allowed to continue and to not let Big Government put up obstacles to inhibit those actions. Thank you. Monitor: Okay Murray your turn. Americans, I am here to show why Government is needed more and more during the challenges of the 21st Century present with the advent of Globalization and the massive shift of manufacturing to China and other low-cost labor markets. This combined with the warming of our Planet and the need to put a halt to toxins being let loose into our atmosphere is a threat to the very survival of this Planet. We need to bolster our Government to enable to have the adequate resources to attack these problems and those on the Right want to cut those programs are in my opinion part of the danger facing us. Thank you for that. Now I would like an assessment by each debater what they believe is the problem with the opponent's philosophies. Okay Victor you go first. Thank you for the opportunity to exposed what is wrong with liberalism. It is a doctrine of giveaway to countless programs that encourage dependency and inhibit the work ethics. Government was not construed for that purpose. Government is only for the protection and keeping the peace. Limited Government is a good thing and promoted individuals to work. The Common Man cannot be trusted to help themselves when they have their basic needs provided. That well sums it up.

Monitor now to Murray

Wow what Victor just said is a total indictment of Conservatism and very dangerous for this economy to grow and remain strong. There have been many studies done that prove the dependency argument false. Most Americans prefer working. Whenever a large company has job opening's thousands show up to apply. What my fellow opponents believe is the masses cannot be trusted to do the right thing. Liberals on the other hand believe in the basic goodness in us all to do the right thing when opportunity presents itself. This opportunity needs to flourish in an open market and not limited to the back room of the privilege 1%. I believe that when hope is diminished by conservative actions, we see a rise in the crime rate and social unrest. History is there to back up these claims. The Great Depression of the 1930's and the financial crisis of early 2008 all point to the very disconcerting results of reactionary thinking that permeates the conservative agenda. Hey Victor, it is about time you guys wake up and join the 21st Century. The debate was pretty much a tie. Both made their points with a lot information. The Monitor thanked both and each had a closing statement It was individuality versus the common good and what had to be supported and funded. It was discussed in précised detail. Both took away an appreciation of each other's viewpoint. They promised to meet in the future to share more for a possible manifesto for helping to achieve a working compromise for further action. It was a very important start of a much-needed dialogue between the two different views. Hopefully it will help with future proposals by either side to be implemented. Dealing with the many issues facing our Nation is so important and must not be put asunder by Demigod's Amen Bubba Paulie The Ballie is center stage with a spotlight hitting him full force. In the darkness to the side is someone sitting on a high stool (hardly recognized)

Hey Bubba, lend an ear. And say hello. to the audience. Bubba responds, "Howdy Folks haven't a clue what is coming so let it rip Pop's

SCENE 2

GREAT GRAND PAPPY'S SERVICE DURING CIVIL WAR

A recent article in the New York Times by David Brooks, titled "The Case for Reparations", is inspiring this Writer to write this play.

Bubba says, "How come"? Well let's look at another time of chaos and uncertainty when slave owners in the year of our lord 1841 were making huge profits off slaves who were the property of their owners through no fault of their own. Stolen from their homes in Africa and separated from their love one's was so aptly depicted in the current film by Steve McQueen's "12 Years a Slave". This film is truly one of epic portions putting the audience through that horrendous treatment of debauchery and sadistic control over another human being. Although Mr. McQueen shows these actions in vivid detail with Solomon the main character in the film, the character never loses his self-respect and holds his dignity for all to see. Solomon a free, educated man from Saratoga, New York who is kidnapped while performing as a musician and taken in chains to be sold at a slave auction is more than riveting it will mesmerize you and hold you spellbound. Watching this movie is a must for every American as it is a history lesson that needs to be told repeatedly for every generation to grasp and hold it close. The ending is very special and for Moi inspiring. Solomon went on to write his story which now is so courageously portrayed in this extremely important film. The Human Spirit is of course indomitable and will as in this fine film endure. So, let's take this another step further.

"Okay Pop's remember your Great Grandfather, William Harrison Spidell fought for the Union as a young recruit from Missouri during the battle of Chancellorsville in April of 1863 and he wisely kept a journal showing how he was affected by what that article showed in vivid detail. (Scene 2) A soldier lies next to his cannon: The young soldier thinks how quiet it is and looks up into the sky to see birds flying high above, in the background he hears crickets chirping and there is an almost no indications that soon a battle will commence. He has some anxious moments but remembers what his commanding officer said, "When the battle is on one will be so busy loading and reloading there will no time to be afraid. So, put aside those fears young man as what will be will be". He goes on to say, "what we are fighting for is the very survival of our Nation. Our forefathers gave us a Constitution that is worth trying to preserve and this war must be won to achieve that end. No man should be the master of another. No man should enslave and debased and dehumanized another. Seldom in recorded history has such a principle been defended for some many peoples". At that very moment you hear a tremendous roar directly in front of you and immediately recognized as thousand voices yelling at the top of their voices It is hard to discerned what it is, but you think it's, "Here comes Stonewall"

You hear the command fire at will, fire at will, your hands are calm, and the reloading goes well for at least 12 shots are done before you feel a great force hit your leg. You look down at the bone is sticking out and the blood is gushing forth. The bandanna Mom gave you comes in handy and the medic uses it to apply a tourniquet. Now Bubba getting hit like this so early in the campaign is truly a blessing for you are taken off the front lines to the rear and taken for transport to hospital to save that leg.

The battle rages on for 6 days and the Union is defeated and General Lee's uses daring tactics by splitting his forces into two forks of assault and causes a wedge in the Union Positions. The Union General concedes and withdraws. Critics will later call him too timid and unwilling to counterattack. .But History tells us although the South had a major victory here, they were mortally wounded losing too many soldiers in the process and the loss of Stonewall Jackson was a catastrophe Now what happens just one week later when still resting in Hospital is truly amazing. It is early one morning. You look up and see a tall figure approaching your bed. His face is something you will never forget. Gaunt but with a very determined look in his eye. He comes to your bed and extends his hand. You grab it and a strange calmness radiates forth. You know at once President Lincoln is smiling at you. He says, "Young man your sacrifice here will not be in vain. What you have done here, fighting to preserve this great nation will resonate throughout time. Your children and their children will be forever grateful for you and all the other young men actions here. Our task is not an easy one and but one that must be done. Freedom for all no matter what color they may be is what we are fighting for. And some day a man of color may be holding this office as I do this day. God bless you and thank you for your service to this great Nation". So, the war continues for another grueling 2years with countless loss of life. Deepening the sense of lost so intense that we as a Nation have still not gotten over the devastating effect that wrath had on our Nation's psyche., President Lincoln realized this and warned the following, " Yes, if God wills that it continues until all the wealth piled by the bondsman's 250 years of unrequited toil shall be sunk, and until every drops of blood drawn with the sword, as was said 3,000 years ago, so still it must be said, "the judgements of the Lord are true and righteous altogether". Any such violation of the natural moral order as slavery was presents a dire blow to decency that will have serious repercussions and must be eventually dealt with so our Nation can move on as a just and moral community. Sadly, to date this has not been addressed as racism runs rampant on Main Street U.S. Another tragic display of evil came about in a small town in Baxter Springs, Kansas in Oct 1863:

On October 6th, 1863. a treacherous attack happened early in the morning on that fateful day. General James Blount and 100 men were camped near what is now known as Baxter Springs, Kansas. They were engaged by the devious Confederate renegade William Quantrill and several hundred Confederates masquerading as Union Troops. As General Blout was preparing a musical salute the enemy let loose a devastating hail of bullets killing over 90 Union Troops. Fortunately, General Blount escaped with a few of his men. Shortly thereafter the Rebels attacked Lt. James Pond and his 95 men further down the road. Lt. Pond put up a gallant response and drove those Rebels to retreat. Thus, preventing another massacre. Lt. Pond would receive a citation from his commanding officer. But on the other hand, Quantrill and his henchman were label as the lawless guerillas and were known to have killed many defenseless civilians in towns like Lawrence and others. His mission was to blunder and kill. Eventually two years later he would be hunted down and killed. Quantrill and his henchman were merchants of death with destruction without honor and not a single shred of human decency. Quantrill would encourage others like Jessie James and his brother Frank to a life of crime. Which strangely our history has been very kind to both. Kind made them look as a sort of Robin Hood. Another example of glorification of lawlessness.

SCENE 3

BATTLE OF LITTLE BIG HORN CROW, MT.

Moving on to ten years after that Civil War we had another sad and tragic episode to show thee; the Battle of Little Big Horn. Okay Bubba are you ready for this? Yup let it fly Pop's The Yellow Hair Curse Okay Bubba I got a theory about the whole thing with George Armstrong Custer and his defeat at Little Big Horn those many years ago and just how just maybe that plays into today's scenario. So, let's get started. Several factors contributed to Custer's defeat.

1. The force he was to confront was grossly underestimated.

2. The 7th Cavalry was poorly trained, and their rifles were only one shot at a time and tending to overheat.

3. He left the Gatling guns at the Fort, thinking they would slow them down.

4. His officers under him hated him and thought him to be a glory hunting self-centered egotist who had no concern for his troops. (Sound familiar?)

5. He split his command up sending two companies to the left flank and the right flank resulting losing the high ground which the was taken by the Indians. This gave the combatants a ten to one advantage.

6. Sitting Bull who was reported to have not taken part in the conflict was safely away in a cave mediating. He had a vision that Yellow Hair his term for Colonel Custer would be defeated and a major victory for the Sioux nation predicted. I can only guess that Sitting Bull who a great believer in destiny was able to foresee the future and his vision was although they prevailed this time the future had disastrous things in store. As history tells us that is what exactly happen, The aftermath the Indians' various tribes suffer several massacre's and were pushed into reservations and forced to leave their lands. A terrible mark on this Nation's legacy. So, what did Sitting Bull do? He called upon the Great Chief to place a spell on all Yellow Hair Leaders who disregard humane treatment of all peoples. This curse could eventually defeat and bring to Justice these current perpetrators of hate and fear; just as it did to Colonel Custer those many moons ago. That last moment for Custer was unusual in that as Custer was surrounded and his troops gravelly wounded and dying, he had this last thought. He envisioned the bullet that was directed at his forehead coming to him in slow motion. He had a sudden realization that soon it would end for him. He had one regret that he did not have a more humane approach to his duties but felt a pride that he served his Country with honor and dedication. As the bullet entered his brain, he made a salute to all his fallen comrades and then darkness fully engulfed him. It was noted later by two Indian maidens who watched this all transpire that he was covered with a blanket woven by them so he would have a safe journey to the after world. And so, ended this one of the most severe lost to our 7th Cavalry.

Surely more efforts should have been done to reach an amicable settlement to those disputes. Amen Bubba Under the Little Big Horn Soliloquy Eager for battle with little fear they followed their Leader to vanquish their foes and anyone who stood in their way.

Custer lead the charge yellow hair flowing in the wind. Then without warning a barrage of arrows flew into their midst cutting down many. A call for halt and dismount to form a circle they all reach for their swords dismally to no avail as they were left by order of Custer as of no use here and not needed. It was a time to die. And when the dust had cleared no one survived. Senseless loss of life with more to come Under the Little Big Horn Is what we mourn.

SCENE 4

WILD BILL SHOW OUT WEST

Now let's set the stage for remarkable friendship that gives hope for peaceful interaction between the races .Fast forward to 1884.

Sitting Bull. Introduces himself to the young sharpshooter. He had been watching her since the early morning rehearsal of the Wild Bill show which was starting its American tour. During the year of our Lord 1884: Sitting Bull : "You have been gifted by the Great Chief. Never missing each shot is truly a skill to cherish. I am Sitting Bull Chief of many tribes and I came on this Buffalo Bills show as a courtesy to him and with need to express the plight of my tribes who have been placed off their lands and many have been killed in the process" Annie Oakley is impressed as her history was also riddled with abuse and a disregard for humane treatment. So, Annie responds., " Thank you Chief we have a lot in common and if we come together during this tour, it will show that yes, we can get along with living together as one Nation. Their appreciation of each other situation was a hopeful sign that the beginning of improve race relations was started. During the next few months they would become the best of friends, Ending up with Sitting Bull adopting her as his daughter. He would go to call her, "Little Sure

Shot". Annie would go on to use this name throughout her famous career. They will remain friends for the rest of their lives. Sitting Bull was later killed mainly because he was deemed a threat This assumption was not based with any true facts and his killing was without merit. Another tragedy that has not been reported justly. Sitting bull was a visionary who only focus was that his tribes be treated humanely and not abused and killed without cause. This failure to recognized him as an important leader for Native America must also be remedied. Got that Bubba, Yup Pop's.

SCENE 5

MANDALAY HOTEL ROOM FACING OUT TO FRONT OF HOTEL

Fast forward to October 1st, 2017. Las Vegas. Another massacre showing that we are still in the throes of self-destructiveness with no sign of let up we offer this possible scenario: As he gently touched the hair trigger with continuous volleys in machine gun velocity hundreds of deadly bullets rain down on our Sons, Daughters, Wife's and Husbands, Police Officers, Teachers, Students and More. Every segment of our society was not spared. He felt numb, no feelings, as the darkness was so strong it engulfed him with such intensity that he was without any concern for anything including himself. Somewhere down deep in his mind he had this idea that soon it would end for him. He did not fight that. As he placed the revolver in his mouth something finally flashed into view a picture of his mother holding him as a small child. Too late too late for him. Some suggestions on just why we have seen so many tragic shootings, we offer this. Perception as defined in the dictionary is the way you think about or understand someone or something. In addition, it is the act or faculty of perceiving or apprehending by means of the senses or of the mind, cognition understanding. We all must make choices based on our perception of the matter confronting us.

How we make these decisions pretty much determines what path we will take. So, the ability to make the best possible decisions are of course determined by how accurate these perceptions are and once made how they will affect your life's journey. Sometimes perceptions can be influenced by people using subterfuge like we see today. Not all peoples have the same perception on things such as politics', religion, truth, etc. These differences are so evident in our current political debate. One must be so careful on what is based on fact and not false assertions that play on fear and hate. Of course, all have the right to express their views, but the real danger lies in electing those extremist's to office such as we see is currently on display in the Republican race for the White House. In my following short story titled, "The Collaborators" I have in Chapter One, "The Encounter", brought two brilliant minds of literature and the Cinema together during a chance meeting on a train in Essex, England in the year of Our Lord 1925 They both are prime examples of using people's different perceptions to create stories with countless surprises that we all have cherished over the years.

SCENE 6

COMPARTMENT ON TRAIN LEAVING FROM ESSEX, ENGLAND

I have no evidence to prove they ever had this meeting but who is to deny it could have happened. Both are English, both are within seven years of age of each other. Our Heroine is 7 years younger than our Hero. She comes from a family of artists and her father was an actor of some note, Gerald du Maurier. Her sister Angela also was a writer. Her Grandfather was the artist and writer George du Maurier. What a background for this brilliant writer. Daphne du Maurier Now to our Hero, a young man on the move. He became interested in his life's vocation at a very young age. He wrote his first story in 1919 about a young woman who has a hallucination about being assaulted. He would go on the write several more stories with diverse subjects. Shortly thereafter he became interested in Photography and started working in film production. He had a five-year apprenticeship and got his first film director job. He would go on to be one the greatest film directors of the 20th century. He is often referred as the, "Master of Suspense" You probably already guessed his name, my personal hero, Alfred Hitchcock. Now to the Meeting.

She was on her way to visit her family in London, The train ride from Essex only took 60 minutes so no one thought she couldn't do it on her own. Her appearance was striking, Beautiful light brown hair that form a somewhat tassel of light when the sun hit it. She was dressed in a traditional suit of light brown color. She was deeply engrossed in her book, When the young man came into the compartment. He was slightly overweight. But no one would call him fat. There was an air of a confident person who was ever watchful of the wonders about him. One could see he was very observant and storing much of his experiences safely away for future reference. He noticed the young women at once and thought to himself wow what an interesting face. Their eyes locked for a moment and the young man had the strangest feeling they met once before. His interest was so strong he could not refrain from introducing himself. To his amazement she extended her hand saying hello. He immediately exchanged the greeting saying something about how great the weather was for this time of the year. She smiled and at that moment a bond of friendship occurred. They would talk of all sorts of things during next hour. He hadn't talked to anyone like this during his life. She told him about her writings, and he mentioned his stories as well. Both were extremely interested in what the other had to say. It was one of those magical moments. Right then a pact was made by these two young artists to keep a watchful eye out for their future works and just maybe they would someday collaborate. And the rest is history they would do 3 films together that become classic tales of mystery and intrigue .Rebecca, Jamaica Inn, and The Birds. What they both shared was the knowledge that the human condition could take violent turns without warnings. These occurrences could happen at any time and to anyone. People of ordinary lives were not immune. How some survived these twists of fate runs rampant through both of their respective works. Both were saddened when the train pulled into the London Terminal. They parted as friends for life and would go their separate ways. Daphne to a marriage with three children to military hero of WWII. And Alfred to marry his Alma his love of his life who would aide him so well with his film's success. Truly one of the great collaborations of all time. And of course, the Director would use his newly acquaintance as a role model for all his Lead Ladies in his many films. Hey Bubba, what to do we cannot move to a more peaceful community when we behaved in such a destructive manner. Any suggestions my friend.

SCENE 7

BUBBA AND ARTHUR MILLER ON STAGE FOR A TALK

Yeah how about this let's go back in time and ask a few literary giants what must change in order to live in peace, let's start with that great Playwriter Arthur Miller. Okay Bubba take it from here. Let's set the stage. A table with a tankard of water with two chairs. The audience applauds as two elderly gentlemen come on stage. One is my lead character Bubba and one is the great playwriter Arthur Miller.

Bubba asks, "It is pleasure to confer with you Sir. I have a deep need to discuss with you what is happening in today's political arena. What are your thoughts on why a man who has the support of white supremacists gets elected"? Mr. Miller scratches his head and replies, "It is very similar to the 1930's another time of uncertainty. There is deep fear that things are getting out of hand and so what if values are forgotten, people are scared out of their wits and need someone to reassure them that everything will be okay. That person senses the fear and jumps right in to exploit those fears. Too bad he is on a mission of death to all who he does not like for people of different religions, people of different races. He wants to eliminate those forces and goes on a systematic plan to do just that and bingo we had the Final Solution ."Bubba now scratches his head and says, "Wow here we go again. Is there any hope to avoid such things like that from happening again?" Mr. Miller says, "Yes, the forces of good must give a voice to be heard that these dangerous times are again at work. Literature is the best tool to bring this out. The writer must sound the alarm. Let his voice ring loud and clear for all to hear. Poet's and Playwriter's and Screen Writers have the responsibility to speak to this with a such force that all will hear. That is their mission, and furthermore never was there a nobler cause, for the very survival of our Planet is at stake." In addition, what is at work here is a malaise of paranoia that is coupled with that already in place feeling by conservatism that the public at large cannot be trusted and must be kept down and under the control of forces in the Right movement. Their message is they know better and must keep the reins to ensure that the masses are not given too much power. It is historically proven that those folks want to run things and make sure the nothing will in fact change that premise. "Bubba responds, "What we see of late that conservatism has abandoned a lot of their beliefs of fiscal responsibility with the passage of the massive trillion's dollar deficit with the recently passed budget by Congress."

Mr. Miller, responds, "Yes the withdrawal from that fiscal responsibility is motivated out of a kind of need they will do anything to remain in control. It like selling their souls to the Devil to maintain a personal enrich lifestyle. It is purely a thoughtless and selfish motive with no thought to the consequences for our Nation."

Bubba says, "I got it! Liberalism is made to be the scapegoat and a danger by the Right with those other foreign forces that have been meddling in our recent election. Gosh it is a scary time and we must be ever on the alert to protect our values. We are under attack in more ways than we know". At this moment a connection is felt by the two and both sense that if society sits down like this and has a rational discussion of what heck is going on currently in our politics just maybe we can start working together to face the many challenges of the 21st Century. Amen to that Bubba.

The audience respond with a standing ovation and the two-elderly gentleman are seen to be smiling and Bubba has a tear in his eye. By the by which also occurred with this writer watching Ms. Miller brilliant work with her beloved Father.

"Okay Bubba what did you learn here"? "It is obvious that in these times that literature has an important role to play. Expressing the need to look for truth and be an important tool in pointing the way for Society to reach at last a humane approach to dealing with the many issues of the 21st Century. That's our mission and we must at all costs help to restoring hope for the Common Man, for his future is in jeopardy and more important the survival of this Swirling Planet Earth".

We also learned here that there are a handful of Literary Giants that need to be revisited and Bubba wants to acknowledge them as bastions of truth and insight: 1. Arthur Miller; 2. Walt Whitman; 3. Herman Melville; 4. Erich Fromm; 5. Mark Twain; 6. Noam Chomsky. All dedicated to showing the human condition and exploring that with clarity that must be listened to in these trouble times". "Hey, are you crying Bubba"? "Yup, sorry". "It is okay to cry Bubba".

Okay Bubba who is next. How about Erich Fromm. Good choice. Let it fly Bubba. The need to look at Human Destructiveness is quite apparent with all the mass shooting of late. So, we go back in time and ask Dr. Fromm his thought s on this phenomenon:

First, a little background on Erich Fromm. He was a major source for countless books about the working of the human mind. He was a noted Psychoanalyst, Social Philosopher, and Author. He was born in Frankfurt, Germany; received his PhD. . From the University of Heidelberg; and was graduated from the Berlin Psychoanalytic Institute. Since coming to the United States in 1934, he has written more than twenty books, among them: The Art of Loving (A N.Y. Times best seller), Escape from Freedom, The Sane Society, Man for Himself, the Forgotten Language, and The Crisis of Psychoanalysis. His writing has been guiding lines for many in all kinds of fields of inquiry. His logic and premises are well thought out and his voice of reason needs to be heard once again in clear and precise details by all His work is very voluminous and a warning it needs to read with several sittings to absorb all his brilliant observations. I will share some of his conclusions to emphasize his suggestions to deter such necrophilia in the future. He takes on Society full blast and offers some idea what factors are complicit in our Society. I quote from page 246-47. "Chronic Depression-Boredom, the problem of stimulation is closely linked to a phenomenon that has no small part in generating aggression and destructiveness; boredom. From a local standpoint it would have been more adequate to have discussed boredom in the previous chapter, together with other forms of aggression, but this would have been impracticable because the discussion on stimulation is a necessary premise for the understanding of boredom. About stimulation and boredom, we can distinguish between three types of persons: 1. The person who can respond productively to activation stimuli is not bored. 2. The person who is in constant need of ever changing, "flat" stimuli are chronically bore but since he compensatory his boredom, his is not aware of it. 3.The person who fails in the attempt to obtain excitation by any kind of normal stimulation is a very sick individual, sometimes he is acutely aware of his state of mind; sometimes he is not conscious of the fact that he suffers This type of boredom is fundamentally different from the second type in which boredom is used in a behavioral sense; IE- the person is bored when there is an insufficient stimulation. But he is capable or responding when his boredom is compensated. In the third in state it is not compensated." (this writer thought there lies the danger) Dr. Fromm goes on to say, "We speak here of boredom dynamic, characterization sense, and it could be described as a state of chronic depression. But the difference between type 2 compensated and uncompensated chronic boredom is only quantitative. In both types of boredom, the person lacks in productivity; by proper stimuli; in the second even the symptom is incurable. Chronic boredom-compensated or uncompensated constitute the major psycho pathological phenomena in contemporary technetronic society, although it is only recently that it has found some recognition." It seems that the boredom-compensating consumption offered by the normal channels for our culture does not fulfill its function properly; hence, other means of boredom relief are sought. Alcohol consumption is one means man employs to help him forget his boredom. In the past few years a new phenomenon has demonstrated the intensity of the boredom among members of the middle class. I am referring to the practice of group sex among "swingers." It is estimated that there are in the United States on or two million people, chiefly, middle class and mostly conservative in their political and religious view, whose main interest in life is sexual activity shared among several couples, if they are not husband and wife. The main condition is no emotional tie is to develop and that the partners are constantly changed. Another and more drastic means for the relief of boredom is the use of psycho drugs, starting in the teens and spreading to older age groups, particularly among the who are not socially settled and have no interesting work to do. Not the least dangerous result of insufficiently compensated boredom is violence and destructiveness. This outcome most frequently takes the passive form of binge attracted to reports of crimes, fatal accidents, and other scenes of bloodshed and cruelty that are the staple diet fed to public, by press, radio, and television. People eagerly respond to such reports because they are the quickest way to produce excitement, and thus alleviate boredom without any inner activity Usually overlooked in the discussion of the effect of the portrayal of violence is that since portrayal of violence has an effect, boredom is a necessary condition. Yet there is only a short step from passive enjoyment of violence and cruelty to the many ways of actively producing excitement by sadistic or destructive behavior; the difference between the "innocent" pleas of embarrassing or teasing someone and participating in a lynch mob is only quantitative. In either instance the bored person himself produces the source of excitation if it does not offer itself ready-made. The bored person often is the organizer of a "Mimi-Colosseum" in which he produces his small-scale equivalents of the large-scale cruelty staged in the Colosseum. Such persons have no interest in anything, nor do they have any contact with anybody except of the most superficial kind. Everybody and everything leave them cold. (Writer note this is the very essence of the matter before us) They are affectively frozen, feel no joy-but also no sorrow or pain. They feel nothing. The world is gray, the sky is not blue; they have no appetite for life and often would rather be dead than alive. Sometimes they are acutely and painfully aware of this state of mind, often they are not."

Wow Bubba, Dr. Fromm's message is showing that boredom can lead to terrible acts by those sick individuals. The last paragraph sound's pretty much from recent reports of the shooter's life for last year. There is hope according to Dr. Fromm, he has expressed this, "I think it is highly probable that even cases of severe depression boredom would be less frequent a less intense, even given the same family constellation, in a society where a mood of hope and love of life predominated." So, the need to make amends is there as clearly as the nose on one's face. Without a doubt Mr. David Brooks has done just that in his brilliant article in the New York Times. It is inspiring and needs to be shared to all well-meaning peoples that we need to say yes slavery was an abomination to our values and must be accounted for and giving those whose lives were affective the due they are entitled to. For in the end it is the right thing to do.

SCENE 8

BUBBA SHARES SOME THOUGHTS

Bubba explains his theory & hope for the future:

So far it looks like life as we know it may be unique in our Solar System; Could it be our mission to spread our DNA to other Planets? Our lives could be an experiment which in order to survive we as a living species must come together and respect each other and join that mission of traveling to other Planets. That mission is a noble one and makes for a plausible answer to that question, Why are we here? I think you are on to something Bubba. Thanks Pal. Hey come over here, Why, O stop come get closer. And if one listen's really close you hear, "I love ya Bubba". Bubba is touched and reply's "I love you too". Okay Bubba you got anything to say to the Folks, Bubba then walks to the front of the stage and says the following, (spotlight switches on to Bubba sitting in the dark)

"We as a people need to voice our concerns about the need to better protect our love ones. We need to take weapons of war off our streets. 2. We need to have a complete background check for anyone anywhere who purchases a gun with no exceptions. 3. We need to vote for Pol's who truly care for the Common Man & Woman. Voting for Demigods who run on drain the swamp and when elected make that swamp even more of a mess is foolhardy and stupid. Also increasing our deficits by the trillions of dollars is dangerous and ill advised. Let's get back in the pay as you go with a budget surplus while still maintaining our entitlement programs, we worked hard for them and to lose them for granting tax cuts to the 1% is another blight on common sense". Finally, reparations for the 4,000,000 slaves held in captivity for those 90 years". "How much Bubba"? "How about $1000 for each of those 4 million Victims." That's only a drop in the bucket compared to the 8 + Billion currently being asked for that beeping wall."

The recent killing in New Zealand must sound the alarm that Storm Troopers are again on the march. To deny that danger is aiding and abetting that evil and must stop at once. Have we forgotten the history lesson that so many died for during the Second world war? We need to listen once more to those who have witnessed that horror once more so here it is:

Today as we see the Nazi flag on Main Street U.S,A, a much-Needed Reminder.

He was only 27 years of age. A bright, eager member of Patton's 3rd Army. A lawyer by profession who got the assignment of his life. Obtain and document the Concentration Holocaust and bring those responsible to justice. He would go on to see firsthand the terrible aftermath of the systematic extermination of millions of innocents that shocked the world. Visiting several Camp's in Buchenwald and more. He saw piles of emaciated dead bodies stacked like piles of wood. The stench of death was everywhere. He became sick to his stomach and cried that how could this have happened to his fellow man. He made a promise to never forget and to remind us all that we cannot permit such a thing to happen again. He is now speaking out that 96 years old veteran . A man of principle and passion of letting the LAW rule and not the senseless killing of war. We should all join his crusade and raise our voices for peace and a humane response in the countless victims that are fleeing from the chaos of Syria He prosecuted 22 of the higher rank who were thought to be largely involve in those wanton acts of debauchery and slaughter of so many . His opening statement called to task those murderous acts and all 22 were found guilty. When asked did he think it sent a message to the world in general that such actions should never be committed again? His reply was yes, but similar occurrences are again in play and that the ICC world court to act is very ineffective due to lack of Governmental Cooperation. For instance, our own Nation is not a member because of Congressional gridlock.

So, the debt that the world has by letting these atrocities happen so many years ago is still outstanding. Today we see bigotry and hatred play so openly in this current election. Have we at long last forgotten those terrible events so quickly. If so the shame of that is immense and cannot be tolerated. So, all well-meaning peoples must vote and choose and reject those racist views . If we don't those terrible events could happen again . Shocking the world once more while it was sleeping. We must listen to this noble voice of one Benjamin Ferencz.

Any message to those merchants of hate and deaths, Bubba?

My message to those hateful folks is this, tomorrow before you go to bed look at the heavens above. See those many stars millions of them sending their light that happened millions of years gone past. Surely, we are just a speck in the immensity of our Universe Then upon waking in the light of day rethink those hateful feelings that all peoples are not created equal and have undeniable rights to pursue their lives under the rule of law. Thank God that the rule of law guards against such evil and no group of haters can take that away. It is our fervent hope that this message will turn at least one away from these hate full thought and actions. There should also be a lock down on the identity of the perpetrator and his motives. Taking away this will limit such actions for the message of hate will be withheld only for that twisted mind to see. Amen Bubba.

SCENE 9

Bubba's reads his letter for his Young Readers

Today on CBS Sunday Morning (3/17/19) there was a very interesting episode about an adolescent girl who sadly took her own life This is a serious problem for our teenagers with an ever-increasing number of such acts, needs more of our attention. So, Bubba has suggested we send a letter to our young readers: So, here it is:

"Howdy young readers, Okay you are just beginning to see some things. You may be slightly unsure on what to think or what career to pursue or what to study. This is perfectly normal and not to worry. There is lots of time to decide and changing your first choice can be simply done after a good night's sleep. Here are some guidelines that I have found to be helpful: 1. Most important guard against the worst thing and that is Self-Doubt and do not let detractor's hold you back. Many will try to do this so simply reject that. 2. Keeping your health is also extremely important to make your journey last for at least 9 decades. I have found that my senior years are very rewarding and is like the whipped cream on a strawberry short cake. I for one found it to be the most creative time of my life. Being creative in whatever field one chooses is what gives us tremendous satisfaction and enhances one's self worth. I advise one to not smoke or drink alcohol. No need to inhibit your body with what have been known to affect the brain adversely killing brain cells. There is no need to use drugs. This life experience is enough of a stimulator and will take it from me, more than enough to keep one in awe. We live on a swirling planet that is held in space by gravity. Today we are on the doorstep of traveling to far distant planets and you will have a front row seat to that amazing stuff. The Tech. Is already in place and it is only a matter of time before man goes to Mars. I am currently working on a Science Fiction Novel about just that. A spaceship manned by robot's that have been calibrated with minds of engineers, astrological scientist's, astronaut's and teacher's with PhD's in physics and mathematicians. They will all be answering to a master computer which I have named Mother T. Their spaceship will be assembled on a space station and will be launched from there. Please stay tuned for that sometime early next year.

In conclusion not only will you have a front row seat to some very amazing advances in space travel but some of you may play an important role with the planning and execution of that. It is as my lead character Bubba always says, "A real gas of a ride". God Bless and hold on 21 is just around the corner and will come in a wink of an eye. All the best and good luck, Love Bubba.

SCENE 10

BUBBA SHARES HIS PAIN

In Closing Bubba explains his pain In closing I would like to share the following: I have been deeply moved writing this play and while writing a moment of grief overtook me. I began a violent sobbing that lasted for several minutes.

This happened once before to this writer on 11/22/63. Another day of infamy. It was like too much to bear. All this destructiveness so heavy on the mind that it needed to be released immediately . Like a pressure cooker about to explode unless it had a way to vent the buildup. Promoting a look at our violent history with so many assassinations and mass shootings. The questions that arise begs for an answer. So, I thought explaining the process that motivated my story be as an analogy and hopefully some insight to why evilness is lurking in the darkness. It is like a cancer spreading destructiveness on a massive scale. So, I have drawn an analogy with myself and Alfred Hitchcock who had similar reaction as he tried to get into the mind of that notorious killer that was used as model for his movie, Psycho. Mr. Hitchcock had to seek out counseling for some of the dark thoughts he had during and after the direction of that film. In my case I had the same reaction when exploring the mind of the Vegas shooter with the help of the writings of Erich Fromm. What I think both of us discovered that this phenomenon is only natural and should be a Director & Writer's case of curiosity for hopefully looking for some answers and leave it at that. In this life's Journey that we all embark on when born is not of each one of us doing. So, we were brought into this life by someone else. As we strive for why and for what purpose does humanity exist. We must realize it is a blessing and a gift. Not to be ended so soon for those innocent victims of mass shootings. Looking to stop these violent attacks must be number one priority of our Society. No more mass shooting by curtailing glorification of violence is the first step . We must elect Pols that care about the Common Man . Looking to their needs and to restore hope is the second step Writers, poets, actors, T.V. And Movie makers must show us the good that happens each day in this great land. Put aside human destructiveness Folks leave it alone let it fester in the cesspool where it belongs. We are a proud and mostly just and caring Nation. Let that message resound throughout this land. Our prayer is that we must turn away from any glorification of violence. We must end our love of weapons and remove weapons of war off our streets. .Also give those perpetrators no recognition keeping their name off the news. Leave that solely to law enforcement It is our fervent prayer that what we write here will be look at in the light of day. Amen Bubba.

A letter from Bubba & Point of Order: There comes a time when over intellectualizing one's position such as progressive conservatism is doing in the recent essay by Ms. Emino Melonic shows for all that although well thought out just how this transform to real efforts to benefit mankind is duly lacking as it is just words with no action. These questions arise and need to be answered by those folks. 1. Do you support a minimum wage of $15 per hour? 2. Do you support a Universal Health Program for all Americans.? 3. Why have you not taken a position on immigration that allows people sanctuary from threats of death and miss-treatment. And finally, why have you not separated yourself from the thoughtless actions of the current populism of conservatism currently in vogue now? Bubba and millions of Americans are sweating for an answer. Yours's Truly,Bubba (Agent of the Common Man &Woman)

SCENE 11

BUBBA'S CONCLUSION AND SAYS SO LONG FOR NOW

In conclusion, the question for us all is "Y" we are still struggling with race relations and what causes us to bring so much hateful ideas and actions of mass shooting into our everyday lives? We could get a clue to those questions by looking at our history. So, let's look at a time when there was little law to rule the day. Our Frontier years ran from the 1800 's to 1900. During most of that time there was only vigilant law. . But one hopeful sign then was the birth of,The Code of The West. This code brought into play give your adversary a fair chance to defend himself if accused of some crime. For the most part this was respected and kept some sort of civility on the frontier. But overall many injustices prevailed and as there was always an unfortunate deed of greed and lynching of people without trial was a terrible act of injustice. Now today as we see the Rule of Law under attack by a misguided President and his Circle of Advisors ; we shake in fear that this damage to our Democracy will become a clear and present danger to our Nation will cause the very foundation of the rule of law to be under attack just like it was during our Civil War. Bubba shouts, "HELP, HELP". Finally, if we protect the Rule of Law and bring those wrong doers to justice, we will strengthen our Laws protecting our Citizens and be in a better position to deal with racism and violent culture that prevails in our Country today. What history has taught us must serve as a lesson on how to proceed. The interaction between white culture and groups such as Indians and Hispanics and Blacks were still with suspicions on both sides. Occasionally there would occur something to bring hope that we were moving away from this prejudice. The alliance of Sitting Bull and Annie Oakley and their lifelong friendship set the stage for better relations between races. And this is needed to be shown for what it is once again that there is hope for improved relations. So, we need to insert the good aspects of the Code of The West into our race relationships and move forward with kindness and acceptance for each other. Sadly, Our Frontier Culture is still holding a firm grip on our Nation's psyche and moving away to a more enlightened race relationship is our mission. Amen to that Bubba, Bubba wearing his recently purchased blue Golf Hat which has this message printed,"Let's make American Sane & Kind Again" raises his voice and points his finger at the audience and says, "What say you"?

Little Miss Sure Shot resting after a performance with the Wild Bill Show

SCENE 12

AFTER THOUGHT: BUBBA TALKS WITH HARRIET TUBMAN CENTER STAGE

Bubba is taken by this Lady . She is wiry and her appearance is impressive. Her handshake is firm and strong. Most striking is the look in the eyes. Strength combined with compassion plus a sense of determination radiates for all to see. Bubba asks, " Ms. Tubman do you have anything to say about my Play calling for reparation for 4,000,000 for over 90 years of slavery"? Ms. Tubman turns her glance away looking to the horizon and several moments pass by and the reply is, "It is only fitting Mr. Bubba to acknowledge that terrible denial of freedom for so many close to 5 score years. This compensation is well deserved and will without a doubt improve race relations and help many with their life's journey". Bubba and the audience give this a hearty round of applause and Bubba has a tear in his eye. He says to himself wow another great moment for all to cherish and just maybe it will be a new dawn of improved race relations. For in the end it all about caring about others and doing something to achieve a better and safer world for our children and their children. We need doers like what Ms. Tubman stood for and yes fought for under tremendous odds. Bubba and I pray that our

Nation will find such leaders once again. Amen Bubba. Then Bubba and Pops, Sitting Bull, Annie, Great Grand Pappy, Arthur Miller, Erich Fromm, Alfred Hitchcock, Daphne du Maurier. Captain Strong, Ms. Tubman, and President Lincoln are seen walking hand and hand into the Light of Day. But wait they turn and shout "Have a great trip and keep the faith Folks and God Bless this Great Nation"!

Epilogue (Bubba continues center stage recites the following)

TRUTH

When one twists the truth countless times
It is surely dubious and a crime
So, let's get off that dime
And get rid of all that grime
One lie lead to more that's for sure
Taking us on a downward path so don't demur
But carry on so we can all be secure in
The knowledge that no one is above the law
Lies will not suffice resulting in many pitfall's
This fall from grace will resonate throughout time
And when the dust has cleared, we will rest assured
Like some crisis in years gone past
Our Nation will endure
As the truth ring's out with a great blast
Its strength is an affirmation
That lies will not be tolerated
With this in hand we spread that message throughout our Land.
Honesty is here to stay and shall prevail growing stronger each day
As the rule of law protects us all from tyranny that is looming
With all these mass shootings and abuses of Ex. power
We say Hey stop this madness without delay.
Giving us hope for a brighter and safer way.

AFTERMATH LAMENT

As more shooting of innocents comes our way
Will something finally be done this day?
As this Congress refuses to have a say.
What to do with this dismay?
All need to vote this election day
And remove these lackeys of the N.R.A
Take them to task for failure to act
Send them packing in disgrace that hardened pack
For dereliction of duty of the oath they were sworn to say
So, let's get to the polls this election day
And cast that vote to let the word go forth
We want a change to take these weapons of war off our streets
At last saving lives and setting a better example for the World
That we are at last a Nation of preserving life
And all have the right
To pursue their lives without fear
Of a random act of violence & hate.

Bubba takes center stage, closing with this statement.

SCENE 13

POPS AND BUBBA HAVE A SERIOUS TALK

He is joined by Pops and they discuss the most important issue facing the World today Bubba says, " I think I got it the most important issue today is getting rid of the bad actors that are dominating the political scene and the number one culprit our current President whose abuse of Executive power is very worrisome and present a danger that our freedoms will be in jeopardy."

Pops responds, " No bad actors come and go and when they depart, they are quickly forgotten and only leave a bad mark on whatever legacy they will have. So, we need to hold those bad actors to another discipline that being the World Court. Joining that group would send a message that we will not be afraid to have all our actions monitored for humane treatment by those folks. This is the most important alliance and would be a major step forward in achieving a more peaceful world. This failure to join is very much like the failure to join the Paris conference after WW 1 This lack of support doomed the League of Nations as the exclusion of the 14-point proposed by President Wilson would without a doubt could have prevented that tragic WWII. Now it is the duty of all writers and poets and playwriter's to spread this word so all will hear. Never was there a nobler cause.". Hey, Bubba don't forget that global warming rules as the utmost danger facing our planet today. If we don't get that under control, we will have today find another planet.

The audience explodes with a roar of applause and both Bubba and Pops have a tear in their eyes

"Okay there you have it. The time is now to better protect our children from gun violence.

For it is all about stopping this mass shooting madness right now.

And to settle that debt incurred those many years ago".

"Y" Warning & Point of Order

I would like to share this. Last night I had a dream where President Lincoln visited with me and we had a nice long talk about what the heck is going on in today's political arena. So here it is. President Lincoln says, " My friend please listen to what I have to say and most important share it to as many people you can. My message must be heard once again. Over 7 score years ago we fought to keep our Nation united and to stop the abomination of slavery. Today we are still wrestling with this dilemma. The past election of 2016 is a prime example of intentions of the supporters of the current administration to rewrite history and restore those state rights over the common good enabling those red states do whatever they want about race relations, abortion, and the promoting of white supremacy. The rule of law and our democracy is under attack. We the people must not tolerate these destructive actions. We are again engaging in a war of ideas that nearly destroyed our Nation those many years ago. So spread the word my friend. We cannot and must not go down that path again. History tells us that path is only one of greed and self-promotion and always leads to a disastrous result. I pray that my message is heard, and we avoid self-destruction by making the right decisions next election. Thanks, Bubba for this opportunity and keep the faith". Pops concludes with this "Let hope ring loud and sweep across this great land once again". Bubba says, "amen to that Pops.

SCENE 14

O Peace recited by Bubba who dedicates it to Benjamin Ferencz

O Peace

As the World looks for some respite
Why are you so elusive?
Lost, lost, lost for now
With innocent's screaming for help
So many in harm's way
And saber rattling is the rule of the day
A time of uncertainty
As mass destruction lurks
A desperate call for rationality
Stay's O silent to our dismay
Will all go down in split tic of the clock?
O listen to this plea
Stop -Stop- Stop, now at once
All merchants of destruction and hate.
The world must listen to one constant voice

That trumpeter for holocaust justice & restitution
Benjamin Ferencz who's brilliant stand for the rule of law
Could bring all to the World Court without exceptions
Finally putting a cessation to all this madness
Saving countless lives in the process.

Just Around the Corner

Growing up is just around the corner
Each day is passed without much ado
But wait how about that first kiss
How about that first visit from Santa
How about that first buddy
How about that first day in school
How about that first marble shoot
How about that old dog Barney?
Faithful to the end.
How about that graduation to the next grade?
How about that first love
How about that wedding day?
How about those working years?
That were flowing by with the wind.
Now we are retired holding fast with a wink
Hoping our words causes one to blink
And say yes you made me think
I have arrived and no longer on that quest
For it is time to reflect & share
This wonderful thing called living

THE OLD MAN AND HIS LEGACY

As time flies by
O where did it go?
Those wasted years
Causes some regret
Please forgive all my love
Knowing not what to hold
So close to our hearts
Was the culprit
So, who's to blame?
Not me say I
Then who is my friend?
Maybe the passage of time
In itself creates this pain
So, what to do?
Use the final days
Spreading hope and caring
Maybe pointing the way
For a more peaceful place
Let these words resonate
For freedom seeking throngs
Our lady with the torch awaits

SCENE 15

CROSSROADS READ BY BUBBA

Bubba closes with this warning and hope for our future . As our journey proceeds, we are faced with some very serious decisions

1. Will we continue to have weapons of war on our streets?
2. Will we continue to attack our Nation's legacy of immigration for all who wish to be free from religious persecution, threats by the death squads of Central America and have a chance for freedom?
3. Will we seek peace and continue to work to that end with intelligence and dedication?
4. Will we continue to apply the rule of law to everyone and bring to justice those who commit crimes.?
5. Will we stop racism and call out all who spread such evil?
6. Will we recognize the danger that global warming presents to the very survival of our planet?
7. Will we continue to overlook deplorable behavior towards women?
8. Will we continue to support demigods?
9. Well that's what on the table this next election folks

10. So, it is up to you American Voter what path we will take. Author's final comment: Writing this Play has been truly a rewarding experience and without a doubt divinely inspired. Just as it was for many noble doers from our past. To name a few: Abraham Lincoln, Socrates, Joan of Arc, Harriet Tubman, The children of Lourdes, Martin Luther King, Erich Fromm, Benjamin Ferencz. Finally, a salute to the Common Man and Women of the 21st Century who need to step up to the plate and hit it out of the ballpark. Amen to that Bubba and God bless this great Nation. One more thing, just today while shopping with my lovely at Aldi's while waiting in line to check out. A customer a large set man was discussing the Pope and decried his liberal positions. He did this in a very self-righteous tone and guess what Bubba you could not let that go by. So, I heard you say this," THANK GOD we have a Pope who is kind and humane. Furth more why is being kind so much of a problem with these folks? That needs to be answered". Okay Bubba thanks for that. I know you are a big fan of the Pope,as I read your chapter of his trip in your previous work. His message must be heard, so we can see to it that hope is on the rise giving to all the message that yes, we hear your cries for help for seeking relief from trouble war zones and the death squads of Central America. Amen to that Pops' and God Bless our great Nation. One more thing if you need a little inspiration in doing the right thing and get your spirits uplifted, Bubba offers this get your I phone and type in Ashokan Farewell in the search box and listen to that Jay Ungar group play that beautiful rendition of that song and without a doubt you will feel better for it. For me it brings this writer a little closer to my Great Grand Pappy who was a Union soldier during the Civil War Luckily, he survived enabling me to write about it, this day.

EPILOGUE

U.S.A Women's Soccer Team Day In The Sun

Onto the field the eleven came dashing on.
Resolute and determined not to falter
They played the first half with caution, but the 2nd half
They cast away that mood and the battle was on
Surviving many hard tackles, the game was afoot.
With head smashes a bunch one could hear those crunches
Some blood was seen streaming down, causing some alarm.
Only made U.S. play harder and it seemed to loosen that team.
To play now without fear and meet their destiny head on.
Making one so proud that we knew at once.
That destiny would not be altered this day.
That penalty causing this writer to say, what is going on?
So many such violations were ignored till then.
But wait the word came out check that tackle of Morgan.
So, the penalty came none too soon I must say.
The kicker was in no hurry, I saw that glance to the side.
That look was calm with a determined approach with a slight hesitation.
Must have confused the tender and the forceful kick hit the back of the net.
A tremendous roar was heard resounding throughout this land.
Just a few minutes later Rose hit the same spot with another forceful kick.

Joining Megan and the team went wild and then we all knew we won, we won.

As the minutes ticked on the final came and if one listens really close. You could hear 250,000,000 voices in crescendo saying thanks so much. We as a Country really needed that. One more thing, Bubba, what say you? "God bless them all and may each of you have a great journey".

Regards, Paul The Ballie

AUTHOR'S BIO

Paulie the Ballie lives with his wife of 57 years on the West coast of Florida since 1994. He has two daughter's and three Grand's. Playing Golf is his passion and still hitting the ball straight but not as far gives this old Golfer tremendous enjoyment He always says, "Playing this great game keep's one active and young of heart".

Not to forget that it keeps one in touch socially contributing to a sense of belonging to community of sorts. This feeling of connection to others during these twilight years is so important The Spirit of competing on the course is the best therapy as one can put aside any of his concerns that may be troublesome as the player's is only thinking of stroking that little dimpled ball into yon hole."

He has written three endeavors which one has been republished with some minor additions that is Under The Palm Tree Take 2 soon to be release by BookWhip.com

And In The Light of Day published by Lulu.com And now this Play soon to be published a look at why we are here and just might be our destiny. Plus, some comments on Main Street. U.S.A. with some glances back in time.

www.ingramcontent.com/pod-product-compliance
Lightning Source LLC
Chambersburg PA
CBHW030134100526
44591CB00009B/649